YOUR KNOWLEDGE HAS VALUE

Bibliographic information published by the German National Library:

The German National Library lists this publication in the National Bibliography; detailed bibliographic data are available on the Internet at http://dnb.dnb.de .

Imprint:

Copyright © 2011 GRIN Verlag, Open Publishing GmbH
Print and binding: Books on Demand GmbH, Norderstedt Germany
ISBN: 978-3-656-43759-8

This book at GRIN:

http://www.grin.com/en/e-book/214266/health-of-software-process-improvement-process

Rano Istlow

Health of Software Process Improvement Process

GRIN Publishing

GRIN - Your knowledge has value

Since its foundation in 1998, GRIN has specialized in publishing academic texts by students, college teachers and other academics as e-book and printed book. The website www.grin.com is an ideal platform for presenting term papers, final papers, scientific essays, dissertations and specialist books.

Visit us on the internet:

http://www.grin.com/

http://www.facebook.com/grincom

http://www.twitter.com/grin_com

Health of Software Process Improvement Process

School of Information and Communication Technology, Royal Institute of Technology (KTH), Sweden

Abstract

This report analyzes ten experience reports about software process improvement (SPI) projects at different companies. Several lessons learnt are listed from each report and used to derive factors that define the success and failure of SPI projects. The generated factors are combined and aggregated. Finally it is suggested how these factors can be used in order to contribute to the health of SPI products.

Keywords: SPI, Software Process Improvement, Health of Software Process Improvement Process, experience report, industry report, success factors.

1 Introduction

In order to learn about the realization of successful software process improvement (SPI) projects, certain success factors can be derived. A lot of research has been conducted to identify such factors [1], not only from successful projects but also from failed projects as they provide valuable insights as well. The goal of this report is to contribute to the research issue by listing and analyzing experiences of succeeded and failed SPI projects including the extraction of success respectively failure factors from overall ten industrial SPI experience reports. By analyzing SPI projects using such factors, conclusions about the status and health of the projects can be drawn. Thus, these factors are an indicator to be able to state about the projects. They can furthermore be used as a basis to derive guidance of how to improve the health of SPI projects. Healthier SPI projects are more likely to be successful, because they are said to be healthy just *because* they better meet known factors, which determine the success of such initiatives.

In fact, performing a SPI project often means using a certain process model to be carried out "*as a vehicle*", e.g. Capability Maturity Model Integration® (CMMI, formerly just CMM) [2]. There exist other models like ISO 15504 (also called "SPICE") and ISO 9001. The experience reports analyzed in this report mostly use CMM / CMMI, which is also one of the most frequently used models for SPI [2]. However some reports are based on SPI initiatives that do not use specific process models. The mentioned models do not contain precise information about *how* to conduct successful SPI projects, but more *what* has to be done from the technical process perspective. This is a reason why advice about the project initiative itself should be given, and extracted and generalized success factors of SPI projects are suitable to meet this demand. In addition, SPI activities are mostly conducted via project organization. This organizational structure comes along with special properties and is frequently discussed. To perform successful projects a lot of knowledge and technics are required, if the project's faith should not be relied on chance. SPI projects are even more specific and therefore need special treatment and guidance. To contribute to this knowledge generating success factors is a proper means.

After all SPI itself is important to continuously improve processes and thus also the products that are developed using the software process. High quality software products are crucial in order to face the market successfully.

2 Research Method

To conduct this report ten industrial experience reports about SPI projects is analyzed. These reports tell about concrete experiences and results from single SPI projects and processes in companies. These reports are searched for at online databases amongst others like IEEE Xplore [3], Wiley Online Library [4], ACM [5] and Libris [6]. These experiences are listed in chapter 3 and afterwards analyzed by extracting factors that influence success and failure of SPI projects. It is further questioned, how these factors can contribute to the improvement of the health of SPI projects in Chapter 5.

3 State of the art

The following chapter lists experiences from failed and succeeded SPI initiatives. However, it is often not clear how to distinguish between success and failure at these projects, because in the very most cases some improvements are measured, although some other targets have not been achieved. The numbering of the experience reports is allocated continuously within chapter 3.1 and 3.2.

3.1 Experiences from failed SPI projects

Experience report 1. The report "Toward Computational Support for Software Process Improvement Activities" [12] analyzes an SPI project at OMRON (Japan) starting in 1995. "*OMRON produces a variety of highly automated mechanical systems*" [12]. The overall target was to improve the software processes. First, the project plan was revised after the project was delayed. Further plans have been missing, although some activates were still going on. The following experiences were made [12]:

- "*fluctuating goals, and the lack of a shared goal among the process improvement project members.*"
- "*no visualized status of the SPI project, and no systematic assessment schemes for SPI activities but only abstract qualitative analyses.*"
- "*poorly managed many different types of unstructured information.*"
- "*unclear role distributions among many stakeholders including SEPG* [(Software Engineering Process Group)] *members, developers, project managers, and top management.*"
- "*hardly transferred technology for new SEPG members. know-hows existed but depended on members' expertise*" [12].

Experience report 2. The report "Lessons learned from an ISO / IEC 15504 SPI programme in a company" [13] tells about the attempt of a Spanish company called Brújula to reach ISO / IEC 15504 (maturity level 2) by an SPI project starting from 2007. The company develops internet applications with 125 employees. At the final assessment some processes reached level 2, but not all. In the following a set of weaknesses encountered by the project team is listed [13]:

- "*Lack of knowledge of the standard. At the end of the improvement project, it was confirmed that the importance of understanding the standard and interpreting its best practices for each one of the software life cycle processes was underestimated.*"
- "*Higher effort than expected. The effort for adapting the project tasks to the best practices defined by the standard was not appropriately estimated.*"
- "*Implementation of changes in the processes and information about them. Information about new established tasks, concept assimilation and the deployment of new manners of working were hindered by an aggressive planned schedule.*"
- "*Project support tools. The implementation of a set of the best practices recommended in the standard has shown that it is essential to have case tools to support the work*" [13].

Experience report 3. The report "Software Process Improvement in Small Organizations: A Case Study" [15] explains experiences of DataStream Content Solutions (DSCS) in trying to achieve CMM level 3. The company employs 28 persons and provides a service to convert data. The goal was not reached in the strong sense, however many improvements were realized and level 3 can be reached in the future. Some lessons learnt are mentioned [15]:

- "*... Organizations could improve more quickly if they assigned process improvement leads or owners who are accountable for focusing on specific improvement areas.*"
- "*Ensure process improvement resources are committed.*"
- "*Start formal reviews immediately. We should have instituted key review meetings from the beginning to keep management not only informed but engaged. Better communication at this level would have ensured earlier buy-in that our approach was beneficial to DSCS.*"
- "*Assess staff process improvement experience. The individual assigned to support the process improvement effort didn't have much process improvement experience. We had to do much more training and hand-holding for the process improvement staff than we expected*" [15].

Experience report 4. The report "Implementing Software Process Improvement: Two Cases of Technology Transfer" [16] deals with two SPI project experiences of two Danish companies. One of them is to be considered (Case I). High-Tech Measurement (HTM) produces highly specialized software and hardware products. The method they used didn't follow any specific maturity model. Instead they defined their own goals and tried to achieve them on their own and with some consultancy from outside. Hardly any substantial improvements were realized. The following lists some experiences from reference [16]:

- "*... professional values of the engineers dominated the organization, i.e. solutions produced now were better than improving processes and competence in preparation for tomorrow. These values were at the very center of the culture that provided the context for implementing SPI. Consequently, implementation of SPI was tough, as none of the professionals would admit that they had any problems with software processes.*"
- "*There was almost no experience in HTM with SPI, and the project managers had no background for understanding that their perceptions were the main obstacles for implementing SPI and benefiting from specific SPI initiatives.*"
- "*The SEPG never established a plan for the SPI effort. The original strategy was to let project managers handle the improvement assisted by the SEPG.*"
- "*... namely that HTM had no champion who could recreate momentum by being persuasive and powerful.*"

- *"The SEPG and its competence did not have a central position at HTM."*
- *"Management was reluctant and provided little support for the SEPG members in the R&D department"* [16].

3.2 Experiences from succeeded SPI projects

Experience report 5. The report "Software Process Definition & Improvement: An Industry Report" [7] consciously does not name the company's name due to confidentiality. However, it is one of the company's software centers at Beijing as part of a multinational corporation. Primary customers are other corporations. The SPI activities were conducted between 2003 and 2004. The target was to transition from CMM level 2 to CMM level 3 till the end of 2004, which was accomplished.

The report mentions, that all engineers received their year-end-bonus, because the center succeeded in reaching CMM level 3: *"every employee's year-end bonus in 2004 was contingent upon passing the CMM Level 3 assessment"* [7]. Another incentive is the ownership of processes: *"Ownership of processes provides significant motivation for their definition and deployment success"* [7]. The report explains that the risk exposure of the SPI activities regarding the ongoing software development projects *"can be reduced by introducing improvements incrementally to a few projects before full release"* [7]. About a project plan the following is said: *"It is better to have a full project plan where items can be deleted in tailoring the plan to the needs of the project. Critical tasks are less likely to be overlooked this way"* [7]. It is stated that the focus on achieving the next level of maturity within a model (e.g. CMM) is less important than focusing at the continuous process improvement itself: *"Continuing process improvement is primary, certification is secondary"* [7]. As a final conclusion the report says that *"knowing that the expenses resulting from not having a process [respectively not having improved the processes] are even higher"* [7].

Experience report 6. In the paper "A case study of software process improvement in a Chinese small company" [8] a SPI project at a Chinese company, named ICSH, is described. With 30 software engineers the company is relatively small and it is situated in Shanghai. The products deal with software outsourcing solutions and the project took place around the year 2006. The project's target was to reach CMMI level 3, starting from ISO-9000. In 2007 maturity level 3 was achieved, which means that the project is deemed successful. All of the following experiences refer to reference [8].

- *"Process improvement goals must be aligned directly with business goals, not just CMMI compliance goals. This allows getting top management buy-in, narrows focus on the key areas of software process improvement. Small*

companies do not have spare time to waste on activities that satisfy either the egos of process engineers or the misguided attempts of managers to increase organizational maturity level."
- *"SPI can't be sustained without dedicated resources, even if only part-time. Process improvement can also be started relying on enthusiasm of key people, who sacrifices their spare time for this, but usually enthusiasm disappears faster than first results are achieved. (...) The rest of the team should have clearly defined goals, responsibilities and time has to be allocated. It is also recommended to gather those people into SPI project team that will be users of the process: managers, project managers, senior developers and testers. SPI project is touching so many daily activities, and it is common to every human to resist to changes. So if the people will define the change by themselves it will minimize the risk of resistance."*
- *"It is also worth mentioning that the implementation of process improvement model should depend on the culture of the company"* [8].

Experience report 7. The report "Software process improvement under duress: experiences of SPI in a town hall in Argentina" [9] deals with a SPI project at Argentina's second largest city, Roasrio, in the nineties of the 20th century. The city's administration is supported by a software system to carry out transactions for citizens as well as internally. A special section, employing 60 software engineers is responsible to for the software. The improvement plan included to reach CMM level 2.

It is stated as very important to visualize the return on investment. Therefore metrics are needed, because only figures were allowed *"for a clear visualization of results"* [9]. The perception of improvements is said to be important and *"should be defined at the highest level of the organization"* [9]. Every user is supposed to be involved in the project activity. This implies to *"work above the local politics"* [9]. The organization's needs and goals should be the first thing to consider and be started with. The improvement process should be continuous, because to stop after having perceived the first success leads to failure. As key factors the report mentions strong motivation and appropriate training, which is much more important than any technical aspect. A strong commitment avoiding a *"they (consultants) vs. us (employees)"* should be established [9].

Experience report 8. The report "Adopting the SW-CMM in a Small IT Organization" [10] deals with a Chileans software organization's attempt to certify for CMM level 2. The company named Link provides information technology services and employs 20 persons involved in software engineering, 70 overall. The project started in 2002 and in January 2003 the company was formally assed CMM level 2. All of the following experiences refer to reference [10].

- *"Link trained everyone in the software development unit on all the processes and roles the SW-CMM Level 2 covers. (...) This helped the developers better understand what, how, and why they were developing software in a certain way."*

- *"Link involved all its software development personnel in the initiative by encouraging them all to choose a SW-CMM key process area, form workgroups to address that KPA, and propose and design improvements, guided by the SEPG. This helped Link institutionalize the improvements quickly and smoothly. Obtaining this degree of participation isn't always easy. For example, rolling out proposed improvements was harder for less motivated workgroups, inhibiting adoption."*

- *"Link maintained bidirectional communication channels between the workgroups and the SEPG. Receiving real-time feedback from people actually executing the processes being improved helped to deploy effective process improvements. To maintain momentum, software development teams must be aware of the initiative's status and know that their opinions are getting serious consideration."*

- *"An effective way to convince everyone of the importance of improving the software process was to have an SPI champion on the software development team. This person spread the process improvement vision from the SEPG and convinced developers to participate actively in the initiative."*

- *"Link performed frequent process assessments in a short time. Because its projects are usually a few months long, rolling out improvements and assessing their effectiveness early is relatively easy. This also helped Link understand the resources needed for the initiative and plan accurately. Link performed three assessments in 10 months..."*

- *"Link defined many milestones in the 10-month-long initiative, reporting status and delivering process improvements and artifacts frequently. When designing improvements, Link focused on making small changes to existing processes to facilitate adoption of the changes."*

- *"Link's senior manager was absolutely convinced about the initiative's relevance from the beginning. This management commitment and support helped throughout the project by providing resources and helping to obtain buy-in from developers. To be successful, every activity in an organization must have a sponsor with budgeting authority. A senior manager at the highest possible level must be convinced and motivated to assure the initiative's success. Organizations trying to perform nonsponsored initiatives won't succeed."*

- *"When proposing, implementing, and deploying process improvements, Link always considered the*

organizational culture and would not adopt any solution considered to be against this culture. The SEPG analyzed each proposal's cultural impact. Also, when assigning SPI-related tasks to workgroups, it helped to let the groups choose which tasks to do, thus maintaining their interest in the SPI activities.

- *The improvements being implemented must take into account the organization's culture. Otherwise, either they won't be adopted or they'll be adopted in an inefficient way, thus affecting process compliance and performance."*

- *"A clear and visible responsibility for process-related activities must be ensured, at least on a part-time basis. SPI won't happen if no one is responsible for it, nor will it happen naturally in everyday work"* [10].

Experience report 9. The report "Using ABC Model for Software Process Improvement: A Balanced Perspective" [11] deals with an SPI initiative at the Taiwan military, that bought U.S. aircrafts and works on the aircraft's software. The detailed context is not mentioned. However, this organization set amongst others the target to reach CMM level 4, although the organization uses a mixed approach combining *"activity-based costing (ABC), balanced scorecard (BSC) and capability maturity model (CMM) into SPI and propose a new model, called the ABC Model, also called the ABCM"* [11]. The targets are partly reached. The following lessons learnt are stated:

- *"It appears that it is very important to invest adequate resource, to make goals clear, and to actively monitor progress toward those goals for SPI"* [11].

- *"There exist many critical success factors for the proposed model, such as effective communication, active involvement, sincere commitment, cooperative teamwork, complete empowerment and working disciplines...etc. The critical point for these factors is to make it operate harmoniously. Everyone involves and communicates with each other respectfully. The management level empowers and commits to the lower level. For example, establish a consensus on related standards via consecutive meeting and informal discussion for a long time"* [11].

The actual point of the last quote is not the list of success factors at the beginning of the quote, because they are likely to be quoted themselves from the original models. Only the last part is to be considered for this report.

Experience report 10. The report "European Experiences with Software Process Improvement" [14] tells about – amongst others – a SPI project performed at Silicon & Software Systems (S3). The company employees 100 software engineers and has a wide spectrum of products. The considered improvement program started in 1994 and is deemed successful achieving CMM level 2. The following lesson learnt is mentioned:

- *"S3 believe that the philosophy they adopted in relation to SPI was crucial to their success. They stressed improvement not CMM compliance"* [14].

4 Analysis

In this chapter single factors that define the success and failure of SPI projects are derived from each experience report by analyzing the listed experiences from chapter 3. In the analysis the factors are if possible always formulated in a positive way, even if they were derived from a negative experience (e.g. lack of training). Similar factors can be formulated in different ways. If a similar factor was already introduced by a previous report but formulated differently, the formulation of the previous factor is set in brackets behind the new found factor. At the end, only one formulation will be considered.

Experience report 1 lists very concrete and clear findings from the initiative. The following factors are identified: 1. clear, constant and shared goals, 2. visualizations of status of the SPI project including systematic assessments, 3. structured information management, 4. clear role distribution among stakeholders, 5. know-how transfer to new SEPG members.

Experience report 2 provides well formulated hints for relevant health factors: 1. literacy of standard / model, 2. precise effort estimation (here for adapting the project task to the standard, but this factor can be generalized, 3. tightness of project plan, 4. existence of infrastructure tools.

Experience report 3 offers the following factors to be derived: 1. involvement of stakeholders by delegating responsibility of specific SPI areas, 2. assurance of resources, 3. engaged management, 4. literacy of standard / model.

Experience report 4 provides the following factors to be derived: 1. knowledge and awareness of importance of SPI, 2. existence of 'champions', 3. organizational belonging of SEPG, 4. engaged management.

Experience report 5 offers the following factors to be derived: 1. motivation of staff, 2. ownership of processes (involvement of stakeholders by delegating responsibility of specific SPI areas), 3. incremental introduction of changes, 4. full visualization of project, 5. focus on improvement rather than certification, 6. knowledge and awareness of importance of SPI.

Experience report 6 offers the following factors to be derived: 1. alignment of SPI goals with (business) goals of the company, 2. assurance of resources, 3. existence of 'champions', 4. clear, constant and shared goals, 5. clearly defined responsibilities, 6. stakeholder involvement, 7. meeting the company's culture while implementing SPI.

Experience report 7 provides leanly formulated experiences and lessons learnt. However, clear factors can be derived: 1. visualization of results (visualizations of status of the SPI project including systematic assessments), 2. communication (of results) to management, 3. stakeholder involvement, 4. alignment of SPI goals with (business) goals of the company, 5. continuous improvement process, 6. motivation of staff, 7. training of staff (literacy of standard / model), 8. commitment to SPI.

Experience report 8 provides lots of experiences on which factors can be derived: 1. training of staff (literacy of standard / model), 2. knowledge and awareness of importance of SPI, 3. involvement of stakeholders by delegating responsibility of specific SPI areas, 4. motivation of staff, 5. consideration of live feedback from stakeholders, 6. visualizations of status of the SPI project including systematic assessments, 7. existence of 'champions', 8. incremental introduction of changes, 9. engaged management, 10. meeting the company's culture while implementing SPI, 11. clearly defined responsibilities.

Experience report 9 offers the following factors to be derived: 1. assurance of resources, 2. clear, constant and shared goals, 3. visualizations of status of the SPI project including systematic assessments, 4. emphasis on harmonious operation and communication, 5. engaged management, 6. commitment to SPI.

Experience report 10 provides the following factor to be derived: 1. focus on improvement rather than certification.

Table 1 summarizes all derived factors. The left column lists all factors in blocks according to their topical affinity. The blocks are marked by a gray background color. Each block forms a set of factors that in some cases could even be combined. The last block pools all single and independent factors. The right column shows the occurrence of each factor within the ten experience reports. Each number represents the occurrence in the specific report, told by the number itself. Occasionally 'stakeholders' is abbreviated "stakeh.'

Table 1 Derived factors and occurrence at experience reports

Factors defining success and failure of SPI projects	Occurrence at reports
clear, constant and shared goals	1, 6, 9
clearly defined responsibilities	6, 8
involvement of stakeh. by delegating responsibility of specific SPI areas	3, 5, 8
stakeholder involvement	6, 7
consideration of live feedback from stakeholders	8
clear role distribution among stakeh.	1
literacy of standard / model	2, 3, 7, 8
knowledge and awareness of importance of SPI	4, 5, 8
know-how transfer to new SEPG members	1
visualizations of status of the SPI project incl. systematic assessments	1, 7, 8, 9
full visualization of project	5
alignment of SPI goals with (business) goals of the company	6, 7
focus on improvement rather than certification	5, 10
engaged management	3, 4, 8, 9
communication (of results) to management	7
assurance of resources	3, 6, 9
commitment to SPI	7, 9
motivation of staff	5, 7, 8
existence of 'champions'	4, 6, 8
meeting the company's culture while implementing SPI	6, 8
emphasis on harmonious operation and communication	9
incremental introduction of changes	5, 8
continuous improvement process	7
precise effort estimation	2
tightness of project plan	2
structured information management	1
existence of infrastructure tools	2
organizational belonging of SEPG	4

The mentioned blocks of similar factors are now aggregated and generalized by formulating single factors out of most of the blocks.

Block 1 merges with block 2 by taking block 2's last factor into consideration: *clearly defined goals, roles and responsibilities*. Block 2: *involvement of stakeholders including process ownership and feedback*. Block 3: *literacy of SPI importance and model*. Block 4: *visualization of the project and its status including systematic assessments*. The two factors of block 5 are not combined to one and stay as stated. In block 6 three factors are merged into two: *well-informed and engaged management* and *assurance of resources*. Block 7: *SPI-committed and motivated*

staff including 'champions'. Block 8 (second last block): *meeting the company's culture and careful communication while implementing SPI*. The last block consists of single factors with hardly any affinity to each other. They are also not mentioned very often in the reports. Therefore, these factors are no longer considered. Table 2 summarizes the newly generated factors and aligns numbers to these. The order of the factors is not meant to be correlating with their importance.

Table 2 Generated factors

Generated factors from table 1
1. clearly defined goals, roles and responsibilities
2. involvement of stakeholders including process ownership and feedback
3. literacy of SPI importance and model
4. visualization of the project and its status including systematic assessments
5. alignment of SPI goals with (business) goals of the company
6. focus on improvement rather than certification
7. well-informed and engaged management
8. assurance of resources
9. SPI-committed and motivated staff incl. 'champions'
10. meeting the company's culture and careful communication while implementing SPI

5 Proposal

This chapter is based on the results of chapter 4, where ten factors to define success and failure of SPI projects were suggested. The following section gives hints about how these factors can be used in order to contribute to the improvement of health of SPI projects.

Factor one ensures transparency about the whole SPI project. By defining goals clearly, assign clear roles to all stakeholders and set responsibilities to single persons and / or groups, a lot of confusion and in general stagnation can be avoided. These three single tasks should be operated right at the beginning of the project.

Factor two stresses that all stakeholders should be involved. Every party has its own ideas, opinions and needs. If some of these are not considered the risk of later disrespect of change is more likely. Therefore all voices should be heard, especially if they provide feedback. But involvement should mean even more. By assigning responsibility, the ownership, of certain areas or single processes to single persons, these areas and processes are more likely to be pursued and also accepted if their outcome comes along with significant changes in working practice. By operating this, progress is better ensured and the overall health of the project is improved.

Factor three implies that a lot of training but also convincing should be done, of course starting before the

SPI project begins. Convincing can be achieved by explaining why SPI activities are important for the company and is so to speak part of the training as well. If people know precisely what they have to do, how their work contributes to the big picture and why they are doing it, the whole project benefits.

Factor four ensures transparency about the SPI project on a meta-level, dealing with the overall status of the project. Thus, awareness and knowledge of the project as a whole can be created and aberration can be identified and avoided. Frequent assessments that start right from the beginning of the project can help to achieve this state. This transparency contributes to the health of SPI projects, because the project is less likely to run wrong operations, being ineffective and inefficient.

Factor five shows that SPI goals should not be operated in a totally disconnected dimension to the (business) goals and needs of the company. The awareness of importance and motivation towards the SPI activities are higher, if a clear connection between SPI and company goals is obvious. Thus, the natural strive for achieving business goals empowers the achievement of SPI goals and vice versa. This improves the health of the SPI project.

Factor six emphasizes the focus on software process improvement itself in contrast to the certification of it. Felt improvement is a strong motivator to continuously improve processes and not stop after having achieved the certification. Striving for the improvement itself should be at the core of project and filled with meaning. A meaningful activity is more likely to be successful than just running for a formal goal.

Factor seven suggests that management should be well-informed and engaged. If important and powerful people in a company know about the SPI initiative and care about it, the pressure and motivation to pursue the activities are higher. The working culture and the striving for success might change to more productive manner and thus improve the health of the SPI project.

Factor eight states that enough resources have to be available to perform the SPI project. Only if all instruments and activities that come along with an SPI project can be carried out in the way, schedule and speed they are supposed to be, the initiative is likely to succeed. Therefore assuring enough resources (man-power, infrastructure, and consultancy) is crucial for healthy SPI projects.

Factor nine deals with all staff involved in the SPI activities. It is the people that carry out both, the change process and the later changed processes in daily work. Thus, their attitude towards the SPI project determines its success. Improving motivation and ensuring SPI commitment improves the health of SPI projects. A key role can be played by so-called 'champions'. They are employees that mostly evolve naturally and can *"recreate momentum by being persuasive and*

powerful" [16] towards the staff. However, their existence cannot be for forced or calculated. If they occur, the health of the SPI project benefits. In general there are two kinds of motivation: intrinsic and extrinsic. A financial incentive connected to the achievement of a certification or certain improvements to be measured would be an extrinsic motivation. To point out the importance and benefits for the company *and* the employees including shared values and visions could lead to intrinsic motivation.

Factor ten suggests to reflect on all mentioned and also further factors regarding their relation to the company's culture. The selection of activities and the way they are implemented should depend on the company's culture to ensure the intention, respectively their effectiveness and efficiency. By respecting this, the likelihood of success of single activities but also of the whole project is increased. A second aspect of the factor is careful communication. The way of communication reflects the level of respect towards the receiver. This is again a meta-level aspect that all factors should take into consideration. Health of SPI projects can be improved by following these hints, as this affects like a catalyzer.

6 Final conclusion

The ten analyzed industry reports lead to an overall number of 28 success respectively failure factors of SPI projects. Out of these, ten factors are derived by combining and aggregating the original factors. Further suggestions about how these factors can be used to improve health of SPI projects are given and explained. A major conclusion is that many factors deal or include social aspects, human-centered issues and organizational aspects of general project management. SPI implies change and humans try to avoid change according to their nature. Thus, change management which mainly deals with social and psychological aspects is at the core of the solution to conduct healthy and successful SPI projects. As humans are different, different companies and departments are different, too. On the one hand this report suggests generalized success factors to ensure and improve health of SPI projects, but on the other hand due to all companies being different, generalized factors are to be used with suspicion.

It is more important to meet the company's needs and culture than to follow strict guidelines about how to perform SPI initiatives. Therefore lots of experience is necessary to ensure success of SPI projects.

References

[1] T. Dybå, "An Empirical Investigation of the Key Factors for Success in Software Process Improvement" in *IEEE Transactions on Software Engineering*. vol. 31, no. 5, pp. 410, May 2005.

[2] M. Sivashankar, A. M. Kalpana, Dr. A. Ebenezer Jeyakumar, „A framework approach using CMMI for SPI to Indian SME's" in *International*

Conference on Innovative Computing Technologies (ICICT), 2010, pp. 1-5, Feb. 2010

[3] http://ieeexplore.ieee.org
[4] http://onlinelibrary.wiley.com
[5] http://dl.acm.org
[6] http://libris.kb.se
[7] M. Jester, H. Krasner, D. E. Perry, "Software process definition & improvement: an industry report", in *SEAA '06. 32nd EUROMICRO Conference on Software Engineering and Advanced Applications*, 2006, pp. 206 – 215, Aug. 2006
[8] B. Shen, T. Ruan, "A Case Study of Software Process Improvement in a Chinese Small Company," in *International Conference on Computer Science and Software Engineering, 2008*, vol.2, pp. 609-612, 12-14 Dec. 2008
[9] J.L. Boria, A. J. Bianchi, "Software process improvement under duress: experiences of SPI in a town hall in Argentina," in *Management of Engineering and Technology, 1999. Technology and Innovation Management. PICMET '99. Portland International Conference on* , vol.1, pp. 404-405 vol.1, 1999
[10] F. Guerrero, Y. Eterovic, "Adopting the SW-CMM in a small IT organization," in *Software, IEEE* , vol.21, no.4, pp. 29- 35, July-Aug. 2004
[11] H.-W. Tuan; C.-Y. Liu; C.-M. Chen, "Using ABC Model for Software Process Improvement: A Balanced Perspective," in *Proceedings of the 39th Annual Hawaii International Conference on System Sciences, 2006. HICSS '06.*, vol. 9, pp. 229c, 04-07 Jan. 2006
[12] K. Sakamoto, K. Nakakoji, Y. Takagi, N. Niihara, "Toward computational support for software process improvement activities," in *Proceedings of the 1998 International Conference on Software Engineering, 1998.*, pp. 22-31, 19-25 Apr 1998
[13] Mas, B. Fluxà, E. Amengual, "Lessons learned from an ISO / IEC 15504 SPI programme in a company" in *Journal of Software Maintenance and Evolution: Research and Practice*, 2010
[14] F. O'Hara, "European experiences with software process improvement," *Proceedings of the 2000 International Conference on Software Engineering, 2000.*, pp. 635-640, 2000
[15] K. C. Dangle, P. Larsen, M. Shaw, M. V. Zelkowitz, "Software process improvement in small organizations: a case study," *Software, IEEE*, vol. 22, no. 6, pp. 68- 75, Nov.-Dec. 2005
[16] K. Kautz, P. A. Nielsen, "Implementing software process improvement: two cases of technology transfer," *Proceedings of the 33rd Annual Hawaii International Conference on System Sciences, 2000.*, pp. 10, vol.2, 4-7 Jan. 2000

YOUR KNOWLEDGE HAS VALUE